Late Arrivals

Late Arrivals

Poems by

Jeremy Gadd

© 2025 Jeremy Gadd. All rights reserved.
This material may not be reproduced in any form, published,
reprinted, recorded, performed, broadcast,
rewritten, or redistributed without
the explicit permission of Jeremy Gadd.
All such actions are strictly prohibited by law.

Cover design by Shay Culligan
Cover image by Alexey Komissarov

ISBN: 978-1-63980-793-2
Library of Congress Control Number: 2025939430

Kelsay Books
502 South 1040 East, A-119
American Fork, Utah 84003
Kelsaybooks.com

Acknowledgments

The author would like to thank the editors of the following literary magazines, anthologies, periodicals and websites in and on which most of the poems in this collection were first published or posted.

Australia
Bonfire Books' Anthology of Australian Verse 2023, *Pure Slush ('Achievements' anthology)*, *Catchment—Poetry of Place (Issues 2 & 3)*, *Arts Rush Magazine*, *Quadrant Literary Journal*, *Verge Journal*, *Sūdō Journal*, *Grieve Anthology Volume 11*, *Literature & Aesthetics* and *The Crow Magazine*.

UK
Indelible Literary and Arts Journal, *Apricot Press*, *Outcast Press*, *Samaritans '100 Poems of Hope' anthology*, *Horizons—British Fantasy Society Journal*, *Rustic Rub*, *erbacce journals 80/81* and *Consilience Journal*.

USA
Written Tales Magazine Chapbook X 'Nature's Embrace', *Redrosethorns Magazine*, *The Orchards Poetry Journal*, *Echoes of the Wild Nature Anthology*, *The Sunflower Poetry Review*, *Penn Journal of Arts and Sciences*, *CultureCult Press' 'Powerless' anthology*, *E-merge Literary Journal* and *The 2024 Poet's Year Book*.

India
Literature Today and *Contemporary Poems Anthology 2022*.

Indonesia
Live Encounters

South Africa
Isele Magazine

Nigeria
Libretto Magazine

Belgium
The Brussels Review

Contents

The Fragile Flower	15
Weather	16
The Vivarium	17
Willie Wagtail	18
Progress has placed	19
Electrical Storm	20
New England	21
Home	22
From This Window 29 April 2020	23
What she gave	25
Poem for PG	26
Snake	27
Sea-mist	29
Where have all the Hippies gone?	30
Fabric	31
The Hedge	32
Singing a fish	33
It is a place	34
The Intruder	35
Gort's Decision	36
Looking Back	37
Artificial Intelligence	38
Come back summer	39
While watching ships	40
Bones	42
To the young	43
For professional performers	44
Arncliffe Mosque	45
Mass Grave in Mariupol	46
Beauty	47
On Learning	48
Yashta 46	49

Then and now	50
Fate is cunning	51
Savagery and civility	52
Premonition	53
Persona non grata	54
Renewal	56
Water	57
The Trojan Horse	59
High-rise rhapsody	60
Duplicity	61
In the same way	62
Winter sun	63
Sic transit gloria mundi	64
Sometimes	65
It	66
Knowing	67
Toward silence	68
The azalea	69

*Give me the gift of laughter
as I lose hold*

—John Betjeman

The Fragile Flower

Freedom grows in several varieties,
often cross fertilizes and self-sows,
and, when compared to subjugation grey,
its blooms are colorful and vibrant.

Freedom's seeds float everywhere
like weightless, white dandelion puffs—
as light as liberty on sunny day—
they often waft over totalitarian walls

and tend to germinate wherever
they fall, allowing dissent,
freedom of choice, always
encouraging an independent voice.

But freedom is a fragile flower
requiring constant attention,
nurturing and protection
from encroaching weeds like

menacing despots or approaching
oppression; for freedom often
vacillates before a storm and,
sometimes, wilts when too warm.

Despite this, freedom's fragrance is
extremely rare, valuable beyond
compare, worth every effort to cultivate
—the alternative is to live in thrall,

emasculated by mind control,
enslaving serf's shackles or
restraining chains and iron ball,
which, surely, are anathema to all?

Weather

And then the rain came.
Heralded by thunderclaps,
draped in diaphanous grey clouds,
La Niña returned, rolling over
land long barren, her cloudbursts
drenching and slaking the thirst
of parched dirt, returning moisture
to sun-cracked soil and,
wherever brown or red earth
lay dry, rain was now relished,
absorbed, until, sodden like a sponge,
rivulets began to run, gullies
turned into streams and swollen
rivers morphed into inland seas.
And as dust turned to mud and
wizened roots luxuriated in liquid
like hikers soaking weary feet,
what were recently deserts bloomed,
migratory birds returned to
deserted places and marsupials
decided it was time to mate:
tanks and dams overflowed and,
as precious run-off was lost down
storm drains, the voices of doomsayers
declaring it would never rain again
were drowned by the raucous
croaking of celebrating frogs.

The Vivarium

The fish swim; some along the length,
some across the width or around the rim of the
tank confining them within their watery world.
Others seem to make conscious decisions:
staying still or darting about without
the slightest indication of fear or self-doubt.
Is there a dilemma of determinism here?
Do those, swimming nonchalantly, believe
in their own volition and that they have free will.
Do others swim thinking they are in control,
like attendees at Davos or the Hollywood Bowl?
Are they aware of other worlds, forces
beyond their small pond—that their universe
has the security and permanence of a junk bond?

Willie Wagtail

Willie Wagtail perches on the gate,
waves its tail like a lure or bait,
foraging for food while protecting
its brood, its vitality infectious.

Surveying all, it searches
for insects among the ferns,
oblivious to human concerns like
envy, cyber bullying, hate.

Darkly cloaked, chest pale,
Willie works its restless tail
while darting here and there in spurts,
feathers twitching—so hard it must hurt—

to one side then the other.
It's as confident as a showman
but does its presence symbolize
good luck or an ill omen?

Trying not to startle or intrude
I found myself strangely moved
by the bird's irrepressible activity.
Its antics, massively adding to the

web of universal energy, lifted me
out of a melancholy mood for
Willie does not know or need the date,
does not care about humanity's fate.

If all ends in climate catastrophe
or lack of food due to a dearth of bees,
the Wagtail on the gate is worry and
guilt free and its slate is clean.

Progress has placed

Progress has placed footprints upon
the pristine powdered surface of
the moon but left it littered with debris.
Discarded lunar modules and rovers;
fragments of spent rocket boosters;
even golf balls, cremated ashes
and the human waste its polluters
left behind, debase the place. But,
from earth, when the moon sensually
rises out of the sea and soars, suspended
among the clouds, bright and ethereal
against the cold, dark void beyond,
despite holding little scientific mystery,
it still remains an object of beauty.

Electrical Storm

An electrical storm rolls
over the harbor at Botany.
Lightning descends vertically
to the land or into the sea
or leaps and surges, horizontally,
from cloud to cloud,
illuminating different parts
of the sky, turning midnight
into midday before flickering
into anonymity like an
unsuccessful bid on E-bay.
Glowing pulses of unharnessed
energy expand and contract
into darkness; the display
making man's artificial lights
below inadequate by comparison.
Planes taking off veer widely
to avoid the disturbed, unstable air
and, as nature's *son et lumière*
recedes out to sea, I am left drained,
humbled by its power and intensity.

New England

As we passed the turn-off to Duri,
which, according to locals, is
synonymous with 'dry', we
were surprised to see paddocks
carpeted with yellow blooms of
cultivated canola but, when past
Tamworth, after climbing the
Moonbi range in low gear, we
witnessed a more powerful panorama.
Whereas, due to La Niña's
recent benevolence, the upper
Hunter was lushly awash and
unusually green, the tableland's
grasses, as far as could be seen,
were burnt straw pale by winter
frosts and a gloomy sky lay heavily
on the land. Skeletal trees added to the
desolateness of the scene, hauntingly
conveying the impression we had
crossed some kind of frontier or
dividing line, and that something
primeval and wild was present,
dormant but still lurking in the
landscape. But after many years
of travelling this route, for family
reunions, christenings, funerals,
there has always been a tingle in
the spine—of recognition—not fear
when approaching Bendemeer.

Home

Home to a tern can be a sandy burrow;
to an earthworm, a warm furrow;
to a penguin, its feet in snow,
standing upon a crowded ice-flow.
To migratory birds heading west,
perhaps to wherever they return to nest;
for fish, the trough between swelling waves,
to stone-age people it was often a cave.
Home could be a rock that blocks
the biting wind or, more complexly,
a spiritual connection to country,
like that which sustains Aborigines,
who reciprocate with respect and
ceremony to maintain their land.
To an elderly neighbor, it's within
the windows, framed with white lace,
that delineate her world. To a refugee,
it's any safe place offering security.
To others, it's where their family long
lived and is associated with identity.
To an itinerant, home is wherever
they find a bed, if not, it's in their head.
For home is not necessarily a location,
a connection or belonging to a
community or being with kin,
for some it has to be found within.

From This Window 29 April 2020

On this day, from this window,
two hundred and fifty years ago,
I could have watched the billowing
white sails being furled, like the wings
of gulls when settling on waves,
as the Bark Endeavour, having observed
the transit of Venus, slowly eased
between the opposing sandstone cliffs
and, entering unknown Botany Bay,
dropped anchor off rocky Kurnell,
where its crew first inhaled the
distinctive smell of eucalyptus leaves . . .

With binoculars I could
have seen the long boat sliding
over the sea before, with raised oars,
grounding on the long-sought Antipodean
shore, where seamen sought respite
from the rolling sea, potable water,
fresh meat and specimens for
Banks and the Royal Society . . .

Lieutenant Cook, who sailed
with instructions for peace not war,
who found his vast way calculating
angles and distances between moon and
stars from a pitching, swaying deck before
being killed by native Hawaiians,
is now thought of as a crook and traduced
as someone who stole Indigenous land:
an imposition of current mores
and values on those of the past.

But then this window was not here;
nor was Port Botany or any pier;
nor Kingsford Smith airport—or
aeronautical engineers; nor the
surrounding suburbs or highways
or railways linking family and friends,
or cars carrying people to work and play.
If, contrary to Rosseau, progress is considered
beneficial, and if 'the moral arc of history'
does bend 'towards Justice,'
Cook's memory will not fade or end.

What she gave

What she gave was delight;
a late flourish of summer
reflected in a glass of fading light.
She had permanent occupation
of my heart and I assumed
we would never part—but we did.
Now there is loneliness in herd-like crowds,
no solace in solitude or watching birds.

Poem for PG

We chat with neighbors, connect with friends,
hire tradesmen, purchase from sales people,
indulge in numerous inconsequential conversations
and, usually, think no more about them but,
what if there is profound purpose to our
brief encounters and hidden consequences
result from our random interactions with others?
The butterfly is purported to be a symbol of the soul
so, what if—like a butterfly effect—when we meet,
discuss, converse, share a laugh or hug in empathy,
we salve emotional wounds and, touching cerebrally,
spread or encourage change, endurance, hope?
For those of us whose labor is for hire and don't
aspire, perhaps this is what we are here for?

Snake

In the cool gully, beneath a shady canopy
of she-oak, paperbark and lazy-leafed tree
ferns, a rivulet gently twists and turns between
water-worn, smooth boulders, as if constantly
replenished from ancient urns emptied upstream.
Sedges lean along and droop down the bank
and saturated weeds waft and wave in the
slow trickling flow—but the dappled light
filtering down is deceptive. Is that a shadow
where the slowly seeping water pools and
meets that mossy rock, spotlighted in a
transitory shaft of light? It moves and
the shadow shimmers but shadows shouldn't
move or is it simply poor eyesight?
It is a snake: partially coiled but long
and slender. Bending and blending with
the almost motionless water's edge,
it stealthily slides into deeper water,
barely causing a ripple as it gently begins
to undulate and, staring mesmerized by
its subtle, sensuous movements,
transfixed by its glossy sleek, black skin
and by glimpses of its bright red underside;
awed by the wonderful creature,
with no thought of a possible venomous bite,
I recalled D.H. Lawrence's description of
the snake he encountered: '. . . a king in
exile, uncrowned in the underworld.'
But how could this being of beauty
be associated with Satan and sin?
Now aware of and disturbed by my

presence, head high, looking left and right,
the snake speeds downstream faster than
a letter 's' could be scrawled by
a pen dancing across the page, like an
accomplished performer exiting the stage.

Sea-mist

The coast is rugged,
wilderness; wild and willful.
Sea-mist obscures the shore;
the sky presses low overhead;
scudding cloud shrouds
the hills high inland.
All appears bleak but here,
in her imperial majesty,
only Nature rules.

Where have all the Hippies gone?

Where have all the Hippies gone?
Did they disappear like unfashionable tie-dyed and beads?
Did their flowers eventually wither, just like weeds?

Hippies believed in individual worth;
that people could live in harmony
with each other and Mother Earth.

They believed in sexual joy not shame
that the abused was not to blame,
in creativity not conformity

and, in nurturing the inner-self:
that souls mattered more than materialism
and, in doing so, created a cultural schism.

The Hippie movement had its flaws
but in chanting the mantra 'make love not war'
it stood up to authoritarian militarism

and, for moment, almost succeeded
in re-shaping Western society.
Alas, it was not to be.

Every generation's idealism becomes jaded
and naïve dreams of Utopia finally faded
as the reality of mortgages and rent dictated.

Where have all the hippies gone?
They're going to Nirvana, one by one.
So sad to see them go, but all must go with the flow.

Fabric

A worn fabric becomes threadbare
and, if stretched too far in opposite directions,
threads will, finally, lose their elasticity
and break. What was interwoven will
begin to unravel, its fibers fray.

When values are no longer shared
and morality becomes subjective,
and the warp and weft of social
cohesion fragments and consensus
becomes unattainable, what was whole is torn.

Shared shibboleths then become slurs
and the accompanying, inevitable, polarization
leads to suspicion, dysfunction and inertia.
Patching with bonding tape or glue cannot hold
hems in place and, what was once one, falls apart.

The Hedge

Within the foliage of the hedge,
birds are busy, chirping, cheeping,
living hidden lives unseen,
while safely screened from view.

The protected birds pursue insects,
while New Holland honeyeaters
warn of the presence of predators,
preventing them being preyed on in turn.

Yellow robins, finches, warblers
and a chime of blue fairy wrens,
creation's crowning glory, preen
or suck fermenting nectar from the flowers

of a nearby red-feathered, bottle-brush tree.
It is a natural aviary, where unique birds,
in anonymity, conceive their offspring
and, sheltered from sleet, wind and heat,

feed their chicks and encourage fledglings to fly.
Do some annually frequent and renew
an affiliation with this hedge?
And when, after their brief lives are spent,

they fall, without rancor, to the ground,
empty nests the only evidence of their existence,
are their deaths perceived as insignificant
sacrifices, accepted by a neutral universe?

Singing a fish

I silently sing to my fish.
Imagining its flecked scales,
unblinking eye, gills slowly
flexing in the rill's current
as it swims in the water below.
I honor it and give it respect.
Insects walk upon my face,
humidity holds me in a hot embrace.
I have stood here for so long
I think like a hungry fish.
I am one with its world.
I am one with all living things,
the large, the small, the wild call,
whether on padding paws
or whispering wings, eventually,
we all share the same fate.
I wait for it to take the bait.

It is a place

It is a place where rain refuses to visit,
where dead souls come to count their pains,
where despair hangs in the air like blimps
and spite makes liquid thoughts obsessive;
where hope evaporates like moisture on the tongue
and wails of loss and chants of loneliness are sung.
You could be past Zanzibar, in suffocating
Saharan heat, with only the muffled tread of
camels' feet, rhythmical as a soft drum's beat
on the blistering sand for company but,
this is fertile countryside in drought where,
dreaming of flooded fields and dams that burst,
farmers contemplate their yields when—
and if—the scorched, parched, land
ever replenishes its long thirst.

The Intruder

A lizard moved into my kitchen.
Not a large lizard, it might be a skink.
It lives either under the refrigerator
or beneath the kitchen sink.
Finger-length when it arrived,
it is, currently, longer than my hand.
How it survives, I don't know;
dropped crumbs, perhaps,
spilt Merlot or insects
encroaching on its domain.
Days lapse without seeing it
but then, announcing its on-going
presence, it emerges and
scurries between furniture.
Initially, adverse to its intrusion,
I tried to capture and remove it,
but—too quick for me—
it tossed its tail and I failed.
I have had to compromise and
come to terms with its presence.
The lizard, these days, shares my place
and I am, conversely, part of its space.
And, now that we peacefully co-exist,
its company has become a comfort.

Gort's Decision

No one doubted his bravery but some asserted
Lord Gort had been promoted beyond his capacity.
With allies imploding, he found himself staring
at the maps alone. When all else was misinformation,
they told the awful truth; the planned attack south
was futile. It was annihilation or retreat to the sea.
To disobey an order is anathema to a soldier but,
after seeking higher guidance—and wrestling with his
sense of duty—Gort didn't hesitate. Aware he was
probably ending his career, he reversed his superiors'
strategy and, although his timely decision became a
personal curse, he saved an army via Dunkirk's quay,
an event which, ultimately, turned defeat into victory.

Looking Back

He looked up but, where the sky had
once been, there was a black hole
leading to when celestial bodies
emerged from inter-galactic slime;
to when the deceptive salamander
appealed to the animal inside the flesh,
when oleanders looked beautiful
but were deadly instead and people
with imaginations cried and bled
and crippled souls took scarecrows into their beds
or cuddled straw men not teddy bears
and extinct beasts glowered in their lairs.
And as intense gales blew storms over-head
the rising dead reminded all to bless
the sun and the bounty of the gentle,
nurturing rain, of treating hypocrisy
with disdain and of precious life won.

Artificial Intelligence

A previous government introduced cane
toads to kill beetles and pests infesting
sugar cane plantations but the toads are now
pervasive and poisonous to native fauna.

To save trees, paper bags were banned
and people encouraged to use plastic—
until it was found plastic was killing marine life
and microplastics endangering the food-chain.

Governments taxed and suppressed smoking
tobacco but then permitted electronic vaping
which creates an aerosol enabling nicotine
and numerous toxic chemicals to be absorbed.

Businesses once used card indexes and filing
cabinets but computerization replaced them with
digital data bases that are susceptible to hacking,
resulting in institutions and individuals held to ransom.

Governments encouraged the transition from
dependable landlines to capricious mobile phones
and now it is claimed radiation emitted
from cell-phones can cause cancer of the brain.

Gas was once cheap and considered clean but
is now an ostracized fossil fuel and governments
insist on the use of electricity generated from unreliable
renewables that rely on intermittent wind and sun.

Frogs have largely disappeared due to the inadvertent
introduction of a virus and the human species may be
next thanks to unregulated artificial intelligence.
Perhaps AI is a better option than governments?

Come back summer

Come back summer, all is forgiven!
Bring back the days of heat relieving
swims in soothing salt brine of the bay;
of perspiration prickling between shoulder blades;
of sitting in the shade of leafy trees;
of the teasing pleasure of the slightest breeze;
of margarine melting when making sandwiches
and the dehydrating bread curling, as if in agony,
under the heat's hot breath; of the slightest
exertion requiring the quenching of thirst.
Even daylight saving had its merits.
Come back warm summer, all is forgiven!
Summer is a hundredfold better than damp,
wet, westerly winds, leaf-mold, this constant cold.

While watching ships

In Sydney Harbor, sleek cruise
ships abound, shuttling tourists
around to loud music but, in Botany
Harbor, a stone's throw away,
weather-worn container ships
constantly enter and leave the bay.

These massive ships come and
go in a never-ending flow,
superstructures piled high with
different colored containers and,
as they pass, they dwarf the headlands
lapped by the waves' white breakers.

Registered internationally
and laden and low in the water,
tough tugs escort them in and out of
port, watching until they're a distant
smoke smudge or nudging them past the
Crimean War era fort, into their allocated berths

where cranes wait on giant gantries.
Rolling alongside on rubber-tires,
they lift the huge and heavy freight,
as if light-weight, from stacked decks to
the docks or onto semi-trailers with hypnotic
regularity and little need for manual labor.

From countries, Asian and European,
come clothes from Mumbai and
Shanghai, coffee beans from Brazil,
flat pack furniture from Sweden,
hairdryers labelled South Korean,
microchips manufactured in Taipei.

The benefits associated with free
trade are obvious and most accept
a buoyant economy provides a better
quality of life—but nothing stays the
same and, as tides constantly change,
so attitudes alter with time.

Some nations are now looking inwards,
protectively closing borders,
building barriers and globalization has
lost its luster, threatening supply-chains.
Prosperity depends on peace; pray the
ships' frequency does not decrease.

Bones

Young bones are usually bold,
old bones just feel the cold.
Walking is easy for young bones,
while standing is often uneasy
for those with ageing bones.
Young bones bend but old bones
become brittle and easier to break.
Bones can calcify and excessive
strain often leads to back-ache
but the same bones are found in
peasants as those sitting on thrones.
Bones make marrow which
replenishes blood and there are
bent bones, metacarpal bones
and straight bones enabling movement.
Bones can, eventually, outlive their hosts,
lingering buried in the ground like ghosts
until embraced by rock and turned
to stone, fossilizing memories
and reminders of past existence,
silent witnesses to lives led and dead.
       The last residual of being.

To the young

To the young, the aged are irrelevant;
nonentities to be pushed aside
as they embark on lives lived in haste.
Most young view the aged with disdain;
seeing them as a waste of space,
ignoring past contributions and
knowledge that could be gained.
Put simply, the young cannot relate.
But why do the young mock loss of memory;
become impatient with slowness of gait
and concerns with arthritis and probate?
Because the young are afraid of the elderly.
Old people remind them, one day,
they too, will be nearing their use by date.

For professional performers

For professional performers,
an excellent entrance is essential.
To be recognized and greeted
with applause on appearance is any actor's wish
but, exits are as auspicious as entrances.
Actors leave the stage when their part is played;
some to the sound of clapping,
others without acclaim and even Thespis
withdrew within the anonymity of the chorus
when his dialogue was done.
Now the omnipotent stage manager has whispered
the cue to black-out and, facing an unexpected exit,
the actor walks towards darkened wings with the
heat of hot lights still warm upon his brow.

Arncliffe Mosque

Like encountering a polar bear at Bondi,
the minaret looks out of place,
incongruous in the midst of what was,
once, a red-tiled-roofed, Federation
era Anglo-Saxon neighborhood,
now a dormitory suburb for CBD workers.
And what does the Arabic text
on the displayed pennants proclaim?
Aren't they the same black and green
flags waved by militant Moslems?
As the train travels slowly past,
passengers stare. How many are
wondering whether those within are
learning to love dialectal reason,
science, scholarship, the freedom
to debate—or studying electrical
circuitry to deliver malevolence and hate?

Mass Grave in Mariupol

The news segment showed a communal grave
containing black plastic body bags, orange
garden refuse bags and corpses wrapped in or
barely shrouded in carpet or curtains from
demolished houses being unceremoniously
tossed and stacked into a long, deep, snow-edged pit;
anonymous bodies, once vibrant, energetic lives,
waiting to be covered by the earth of their birth.
Nothing indicated the cause for which they died
but, as the camera panned away, a glimpse of
the exhausted grave diggers in the background,
risking their own deaths to bury bodies under shellfire,
captured my horrified stare. Between them, in a
blanket, they swung the slender shape of a child,
torso and head covered but its thin malnourished
legs visible, still clad in colorful patterned socks
and clean, white shoes that, only weeks previously,
might have happily been playing hopscotch or dancing.

Beauty

Whether a work of art, personality,
a stupendous view or sublime sound
evoking tears of pleasure, the perception
of beauty inspires an emotional reaction.
Even the transparency of innocence is a kind of beauty.
But why is it beauty evokes such a response,
what Lacan called *jouissance?*
What can be construed from such appreciation?
Are we so used to ugliness, irregularity,
that, when presented with symmetry or harmony,
the recognition shocks and moves us?
Is it empathy, ecstasy, catharsis,
or simply the need to believe in or
longing and hope of a better world?

On Learning

On learning Saul had fallen on his sword,
the Bible claims David sang and lamented even
the mighty are not exempt from falling from favor.
Some deservedly: Hitler, Napoleon, Caligula, the list is long.
Mussolini, hung upside down, after death, for all to see;
Nixon, Head of State, became political pariah after
                                         Watergate.
Some not so deservedly: Churchill's ignominious
defeat by Attlee towards the end of World War Two
Rembrandt bankrupt and reduced to living on herring;
the apocryphal story of Justinian blinding poor Belisarius,
who then begged with his wooden platter from those
he had once protected, at Porta Pinciana's door.
Life can often be unfair and injustices, for both
great and small, something to accept and bear.

Yashta 46

It is said a prophet is treated with honor
everywhere—except within their own country.
Zoroaster, proponent of individual choice,
who preached love of the light and to think
good thoughts, to utter considerate words,
perform charitable deeds and championed
justice, morality, monotheism and duality,
was forced to flee from family and community.
Simultaneously perpetuating his memory,
Yashta forty-six, in the Gathas, records his misery,
his flight into exile, his heart-felt lament:
Where do I go? Who will accept me?
The perennial plea of the refugee,
incessantly reverberating through history.

Then and now

In Sydney's Domain, where, pre-war,
in nineteen-thirty-four, eighteen thousand
once listened to the warnings of Egon Kisch;
where, on Sundays, Webster promoted
free speech and would-be politicians,
proselytizers and the deranged stood
and harangued gawking crowds, hecklers
and the impressionable from milk crates;
debating the benefits of democracy,
the booming or bearish economy,
promising Marxism or Lucifer could change the world;
that Jesus would bring ever-lasting life;
that lizard-like humans controlled the ruling class
and Macquarie Street's decisions were a farce—
young office workers work-out while on
lunch breaks, hoping exercise can delay
time's decay, and all is subdued and sedate.
Some skateboard by, others throw frisbees,
which spin as high as the meristem
foliage of the towering palms,
bursting like flak above the canopy of
the Moreton Bay fig-trees while cars
reverentially crawl along Hospital Road
and suited men carry coffees and stride
towards Parliament House or the courts.
There are some clouds in the far distance
and, as the bright sunshine fades and the
afternoon chills, the still air seems foreboding.

Fate is cunning

Fate is cunning, fate is cruel,
the Spinners snigger at the squirming fool
whose destiny they spin and measure
as if inflicting pain for pleasure.
Like an insect impaled by a pin,
whoever dares fall in love, late
in life, with hounds from Hades
snapping at their heels, tempts the Fates,
encourages cemetery statues to guffaw
at any attempt to deny the trip from Styx's shore.
But some believe that which went before
was all a waste of time and preparation for;
and whatever time is left so precious that
a minute, now, is worth a year or more.

Savagery and civility

As depravity was celebrated and feted,
the ravine between savagery and civility
widened and became a chasm,
a gulf no dove could span.
Cultures clashed and all the lies
and false promises were revealed.
Where once there was unity,
now there is no community,
only mutual suspicion, loathing and fear.
The golden calf of 'cultural pluralism'
has been shown to be a chimera,
based-lead neo-tribalism beneath a thin coating
of glittering gilt and, as hands hover over sword hilts,
the silent majority's silence is indicative of its guilt.

Premonition

When the shot that reverberated around
the euro-centric world was fired at Sarajevo,
and the order to mobilize approved
by statesmen in Austria, Germany, France
and Russia, the wheels of the locomotives
and carriages carrying troops to the borders
began to turn in accordance with long held
plans, an inexorable momentum,
driven by timetables and the cutting
edge technology of the time, took hold,
and a horrendous war became inevitable.
Does artificial intelligence, with its
absence of human input, autonomous
algorithms, portend a similar disaster?

Persona non grata

An elderly white male,
not seeking veneration
but becoming frail, bends
before a gale of vilification
from a younger generation
—which, as his own—owed
all to those who went before.

Feeling disgraced and displaced,
he watches as statues are defaced
while gender bender pronouns
become compulsory and
'sensitivity readers' re-write
books deemed offensive to
more refined sensibilities.

While enjoying the fruits of
the culture he helped uphold,
its stability, its wealth—thanks
to freedom of speech and
parliamentary democracy—
he learns the young lean more
to Marx and finds his values
considered archaic, that he is
seen as a fraud and abhorred and
that, within his own society,
he is now persona non grata.

Intergenerational conflict is long-
established but sensible societies
venerate the wisdom of the aged
while harnessing youth's vitality.
Undermining the foundations
supporting a cultural structure is
rash, and ageism and failure
to accept the past may impair and,
sadly, vitiate and abate the future.

Renewal

There are so many seeking unicorns,
searching for antidotes to personal poisons,
antivenoms for being treated with scorn
and disdain; medical, financial, emotional
procaine to deal with past or present pain.
Some shellfish coat nacre over irritants
but, similar to cicadas shedding their shells,
deciduous trees their shriveling leaves,
crayfish and crabs their carapace
or human bones, which replace
themselves every decade and enable
physical growth—so compassion and kindness
become balm for sores, ointments to
restore the dismayed and betrayed.

Water

*(Written after viewing water-inspired artist
Ralph Kerle's Impressions of a Turner Landscape)*

Shapeless but capable of all shapes,
water wraps the world in a liquid embrace,
shape shifts to vapor or to ice,
creating rain or holding vessels like a vice.

Water emerged from a Hadean world,
when Creation's breath gently blew
and cooled the surface of the seas
creating ripples, waves, tsunamis.

We are one with water: mainly
fluid, our cellular ancestors
emerged wet upon the land before
growing limbs upon the sand

and, as essential to life as air,
water is adaptable, flexible; finding
routes of least resistance to the sea,
it travels daunting distances to be free.

Water symbolizes purity: souls are
ritually shrived from sanctified bowls and,
more prosaically, we wash in water and
luxuriate in baths to sooth sore muscles.

Shamans read messages within water's
dark whirlpools, its eddies of darkness;
its turbulent, tormented, corkscrews,
resembling distressed states of mind.
But is anything actually what it seems?

Like the artist, manipulating what we see,
there is the possibility water crystals
can change shape dynamically
and, if exposed to pleasant music,
positive words—or even thoughts—will be
perfectly formed but, if subjected
to negative energy, are ugly or deformed.

Whether true or false, one thing is certain,
fouling sources of fresh water and treating
the sea as a pigsty will be the final curtain.
    Without clean water all life dies.

The Trojan Horse

The ocean walls once seemed wide enough
to discourage and deter any enemy.
The distance was great, the sea deep and
our isolation contributed to a sense of safety.
But then the wooden horse appeared:
noble, magnificent, it appeared harmless.
A pious plaque proclaimed peace and
the benefits of diversity and inclusion
and, impressed by its promises,
we dragged it inside our wet walls but,
in the night, educational indoctrination, moral
equivalence and disinformation emerged,
infiltrating our defenses and social cohesion.
Too late, we found the enemy was ensconced within.

High-rise rhapsody

We may be only window-cleaners to you
but, to others, we are high-rise gurus.
Hanging suspended in our safety harness
we handle our squeegees with rhythmic finesse;
there is no margin for negligence
when you're twenty-four floors above the pavement.
As we lower ourselves down buildings' sides
with hermetically sealed windows to prevent suicides,
we see human nature at work,
from those who preside, to humble clerk;
humanity jubilant, in humor, stress,
stitched-up or in a state of undress,
and though stared at as oddities by those inside,
from where we sit the world is wide
and we are part of the big picture—
not locked up inside like a prisoner.
From our modern, high-tech Helicon,
we can observe the curve of the horizon
and, like a camera in a circling satellite,
discern where the Earth meets the Heavens and
unites; and from our vantage point we see
that, if we were to fall, we would soar
free before finally meeting our destiny.

Duplicity

In Baiae, on the edge of the Bay of Naples,
Nero's and Severus' palatial villas
have long since sunk into the sea.
Their remnants, due to Bradyseism,
now merely curiosities, mired
in mud, fragments of what had been.
Similarly, in Australia's national capital,
a slow subsidence can also be seen.
National honor has been re-cast,
converted to subservience as servile and
disingenuous politicians, surreptitiously and
covertly queue to kowtow to the C.C.P.;
their obsequious and treacherous behavior
harbingering the eclipse of democracy.

In the same way

In the same way Egyptian priests
predicted and prayed for the flooding
of the Nile and its annual inundation of
fields to nourish the growth of barley
and emmer and avoid famine, sometimes
resorting to sacrifice to appease the
relevant gods should the river fail,
which, as Cleopatra learnt, could cause
civil chaos and the downfall of society:
in the same manner as Mesoamerican
Mayans offered human lives to Chac,
their rain god, to ensure rain came and, with it,
the blessing of maize and other sustaining grain;
the cult of climate change sacrifices in vain.

Winter sun

Motionless in the winter sun
the old, the loveless and those
lacking kin, sit alone, patiently
waiting for someone, something
or merely for the warmth of spring.
Perhaps they wait for meals on wheels
while they vacantly click their heels?
Perhaps, they simply wait for hate
and enmity to abate or are they
waiting for their skulls to grin so
they can become one with oblivion?
Their situation is akin to being
told there is no room at the inn.
The winter sun may heat their
skin but not their aching bones—
nor will it heal the skeletal, deep,
eternal emptiness they feel.
And, what if, whatever they
wait for does not come?
Perhaps their lives have become
so devoid of fun they would prefer
a loaded gun to waiting in the cold.

Sic transit gloria mundi

Time is a termite devouring my days,
denying me longevity and repeatedly
telling me, eventually, nothing
can save me from ceasing to be.
Time is a mirror in which I see
my wrinkles constantly reminding me
of my transitory grip on existence.
Mornings merge into afternoons,
my days are measured in coffee spoons
and summer soon turns into winter.
So, faced with anno domino,
I watch the kites wheel in the sky,
trying to imprint the image on my mind
as if storing it for recall after I die.

Sometimes

Sometimes it's as faint as a
dashboard lock-light or a firefly
in erratic night flight.
Sometimes it's a steady glow,
sometimes it dims,
sometimes it sings
in mantras and uplifting hymns.
Sometimes it flickers, fades and dies
to reappear in another guise.
If hope is the answer to despair,
let it be found everywhere.

It

It always comes late at night,
shape-shifting through the darkness,
avoiding any source of light
by hiding in the shadows.
Its face is featureless,
a document redacted and,
whenever I see it, I have no fear
but, when I reach to touch it, it's not there.
Who or what is it? Why does it appear?
Is it part of the past or to become?
It never speaks but its spectral
presence makes me numb.
Why does it beckon me?
Why do I say, I'll come?

Knowing

Knowing I am soon to succumb,
I have never felt so much in love
with life, with what is ordinary;
with what would normally be taken
for granted: the common sight of
bushes bowing before a breeze;
the ambient buzzing of insects
industrially busy in foliage and ferns.
Even the everyday drone of aircraft,
the trundle of trains and traffic have music
and the monotony of daily routines,
gives me an unprecedented high.
Knowing there is nothing to come,
the mundane elates and excites me.

Toward silence

Like an un-watered, withered plant,
a battery running down, a waning moon
or the abating swell of waves on an ebbing tide,
I relentlessly move toward silence while life,
in all its variety, garishness, complexity—
like a lengthy Bayeux tapestry—rolls on.
Should I feel cheated or angry about
interfacing with mortality? Missing out on
futurity? It is like being on a roller-coaster
knowing the end of the ride will never
be seen, that someone else will enjoy it.
Whether brief or granted reasonable longevity,
how could anyone fail to laud and extol
the gift, the privilege of sentient existence?

The azalea

The azalea beside the front door is ablaze
with color in the early morning sunshine;
each delicate, fine-leafed petal a subtle
combination of multiple hues; from white-
veined with pink to impressionist, pointillist
sprays of deep mauve and purple, like splattered
paint upon a clean palette; its flowers en masse
are resplendent; its multiple stamens, tipped
with pollen, arch and stretch like worshippers
towards the sun, inviting bees and insects to
indulge in its nectar, as observers in its loveliness.
But the leaves and honey from azaleas are toxic and
bouquets in black vases once interpreted as death threats.
If so, let it be the last thing I see as I leap into eternity.

About the Author

Jeremy Gadd is an Australian author and poet who has published over 300 poems in periodicals and literary magazines in Australia, the USA, England, Scotland, Wales, Ireland, Canada, New Zealand, Germany, Austria, Belgium, Indonesia, Malaya, South Africa, Sweden, Nigeria, and India.

His poetry has previously been collected in five publications, including a *livre d' artiste* with engravings by P. John Burden (Bournehall Press, England). Copies of this work may now be found in rare book collections, including the Victoria and Albert Museum in London, the Samuel Paley Library, Temple University, Philadelphia, and the Reid Library in Western Australia. He has also published two novels, two volumes of short stories, and a book of theatrical anecdotes based on his experiences while working in professional theatre in Australia and the UK.

A graduate of Australia's National Institute of Dramatic Art, Jeremy has Master of Arts with Honors and PhD degrees from the University of New England. He lives and writes in an old Federation era house overlooking Botany Bay, the birthplace of modern Australia.

Further information can be found at:
jeremygaddpoet.com

www.ingramcontent.com/pod-product-compliance
Lightning Source LLC
Chambersburg PA
CBHW071333190426
43193CB00041B/1760